Mel Bay Presents

O'CAROLAN'S TUNES FOR PIANO

by Richard Voss and Laurence Traiger

Visit us on the Web at www.melbay.com — E-mail us at email@melbay.com

Contents

Introduction

Turlough O'Carolan (Toirdhealbhach Ó Cearbhalláin) was born in 1670 in County Meath, Ireland where his father worked for the MacDermott Roe family. The lady of the estate, Mrs. MacDermott Roe, took an active interest in the musical education of young Turlough. At the age of eighteen, after having lost his sight as a result of small pox, he was apprenticed by Mrs. MacDermott Roe to a harpist. Three years later, she sent the young man on his way with a harp, a horse, some money and a guide.

Carolan's first benefactor, George Reynolds, encouraged the young man to compose songs, since Carolan, having had a late start in his musical education, was not an accomplished instrumentalist. Early in his career he wrote his first song, "Sheebeg and Sheemore", one of his most popular compositions.

Carolan developed a personal style, containing melodic elements of Irish folk music, courtly harp music and Italian baroque music. Most of his compositions are dedicated to his benefactors and patronesses. A title such as "Planxty Irwin" probably implied "To the honour of Mr. Irwin."

After forty-five years of travel throughout Ireland, Carolan returned in ill health to Mrs. MacDermott Roe. Legend has it that after a welcoming toast, Carolan played his last composition, "Carolan's Farewell to Music" and laid down to die.

Carolan's music was not published during his lifetime; therefore, various versions of his melodies have been handed down. It is also not known how he accompanied his melodies. Richard Voss has compiled Carolan's songs from various sources. Laurence Traiger provided easily playable, lively piano arrangements. Dynamics and phrasing have been left to the discretion of the performer. Included in this collection are three original melodies by Richard Voss inspired by, and in the style of the early master.

Richard Voss & Laurence Traiger

1. Blind Mary

Andante

M: Turlough O'Carolan, arr. by Laurence Traiger

2. Miss MacDermott

Allegretto

M: Turlough O'Carolan, arr. by L. Traiger

3. Miss MacMurray

Allegretto

M: Turlough O'Carolan, arr. by L. Traiger

6

4. Planxty Drew

Allegretto

M: Turlough O'Carolan, arr. by L. Traiger

5. Sir Charles Coote

Vivace

M: Turlough O'Carolan, arr. by L. Traiger

6. Lady Wrixon

Allegretto

M: Turlough O'Carolan, arr. by L. Traiger

7. Carolan's Nightcap

You may play "Carolan's Nightcap" and "Lady Gethin" as a set!

10

8. Lady Gethin

M: Turlough O'Carolan, arr. by L. Traiger

9. Mrs. Owen's Delight

Andantino

M: Trad. from Wales, arr. by L. Traiger

You may play "Mrs. Owen's Delight" and "Eleanor Plunkett" as a set!

10. Eleanor Plunkett

Andantino

M: Turlough O'Carolan, arr. by L. Traiger

11. Thomas Morres Johnes

Allegretto

M: Turlough O'Carolan, arr. by L. Traiger

12. Miss Goulding

M: Turlough O'Carolan, arr. by L. Traiger

Allegretto

13. Mrs. Maxwell *(First Air)*

Vivace

M: Turlough O'Carolan, arr. by L. Traiger

16

14. One Bottle More

Vivace

M: Turlough O'Carolan, arr. by L. Traiger

15. Fanny Power

Grazioso

M: Turlough O'Carolan, arr. by L. Traiger

16. Planxty Sweeney

M: Turlough O'Carolan, arr. by L. Traiger

19

17. James Plunkett

M: Turlough O'Carolan, arr. by L.Traiger

Moderato

18. Father Brian MacDermott Roe

Andante

M: Turlough O'Carolan, arr. by L.Traiger

19. Ode To Whiskey

Allegretto

M: Turlough O'Carolan, arr. by L.Traiger

22

20. Sheebeg And Sheemore

M: Turlough O'Carolan, arr. by L. Traiger

Andantino

'Sheebeg And Sheemore' is said to be Carolan's first composition.

21. Planxty Otto

Moderato

M: R. Voss, arr. by L.Traiger

22. Good Neighbourhood

Moderato

M: R. Voss, arr. by L. Traiger

23. Bridget Cruise (Second Air)

M: Turlough O'Carolan, arr. by L. Traiger

You may play the second air and the third air of "Bridget Cruise" as a set!

24. Bridget Cruise (Third Air)

Andante

M: Turlough O'Carolan, arr. by L. Traiger

25. Planxty Burke

Moderato

M: Turlough O'Carolan, arr. by L. Traiger

28

You may play "Panxty Burke" and "Planxty O'Carolan" as a set!

26. Planxty O'Carolan

M: R. Voss, arr. by L. Traiger

27. Isabella Burke

M: Turlough O'Carolan, arr. by L. Traiger

28. Cremonea

Andante

M: Turlough O'Carolan, arr. by L. Traiger

29. Squire Parsons

Andante

M: Turlough O'Carolan, arr. by L. Traiger

30. The Clergy's Lamentation

Moderato

M: Turlough O'Carolan, arr. by L. Traiger

31. Planxty Maggie Browne

Andante moderato

M: Turlough O'Carolan, arr. by L. Traiger

32. Lament for Owen Roe O'Neill

M: Turlough O'Carolan, arr. by L. Traiger

33. Captain Sudley

Moderato

M: Turlough O'Carolan, arr. by L. Traiger

34. Carolan's Concerto

Allegro

M: Turlough O'Carolan, arr. by L. Traiger

35. Carolan's Patronesses

M: Turlough O'Carolan, arr. by L. Traiger

Made in the USA
Lexington, KY
28 June 2013